The Crimean War

The Crimean War, 1853-56

by

G.A. Embleton

ALMARK PUBLISHING CO. LTD. LONDON

First published 1975

ISBN 0 85524 242 6 (paper cover)
ISBN 0 85524 243 4 (hard cover)

Printed in Great Britain by
Pan Litho Ltd.,
Pan House, 172-176, The Highway,
London E1 9DD,
for the publishers, Almark Publishing Co. Ltd.,
49 Malden Way, New Malden,
Surrey KT3 6EA, England.

Contents

Acknowledgement

The author would like to thank the library and photographic staff of the National Army Museum for their usual very kind assistance; Ron Harris for supplying photographs from his magnificent collection at a rather awkward time; Martin Windrow for reference material on the French Army.

Foreword

The Crimean War 1853-6 was the first major outbreak among the great powers of Europe after the Napoleonic Wars at the beginning of the century. Many verdicts have been passed on it by hosts of commentators, interpreters and apologists. In spite of the emotive appeal of some of the actions in which British troops participated, one is struck by a certain lack of enthusiasm in these judgments, by the several undoubted question marks that hang over aims, preparedness and performance, by the use of descriptions like "an unnecessary war", and of epithets like "disappointing" and "unsatisfactory".

In view of the difficulty in assessing or evaluating all the relevant economic, material, moral and humanitarian considerations, it is foolhardy to attempt a really convincing definition of a "satisfactory war". Similarly, a short account of any major international conflict might sound presumptuous, so strongly is the deeply ingrained habit of warfare surrounded by irrational and imponderable considerations, as well as by plain aggressiveness and self seeking. However, one thing is certain in the Crimean War; the number of soldiers and their deployment, their equipment and supply problems, the terrain and the weather are aspects of the reality of war that even a brief account can record with some accuracy and, it is hoped, with justice to all the fighting men, on both sides.

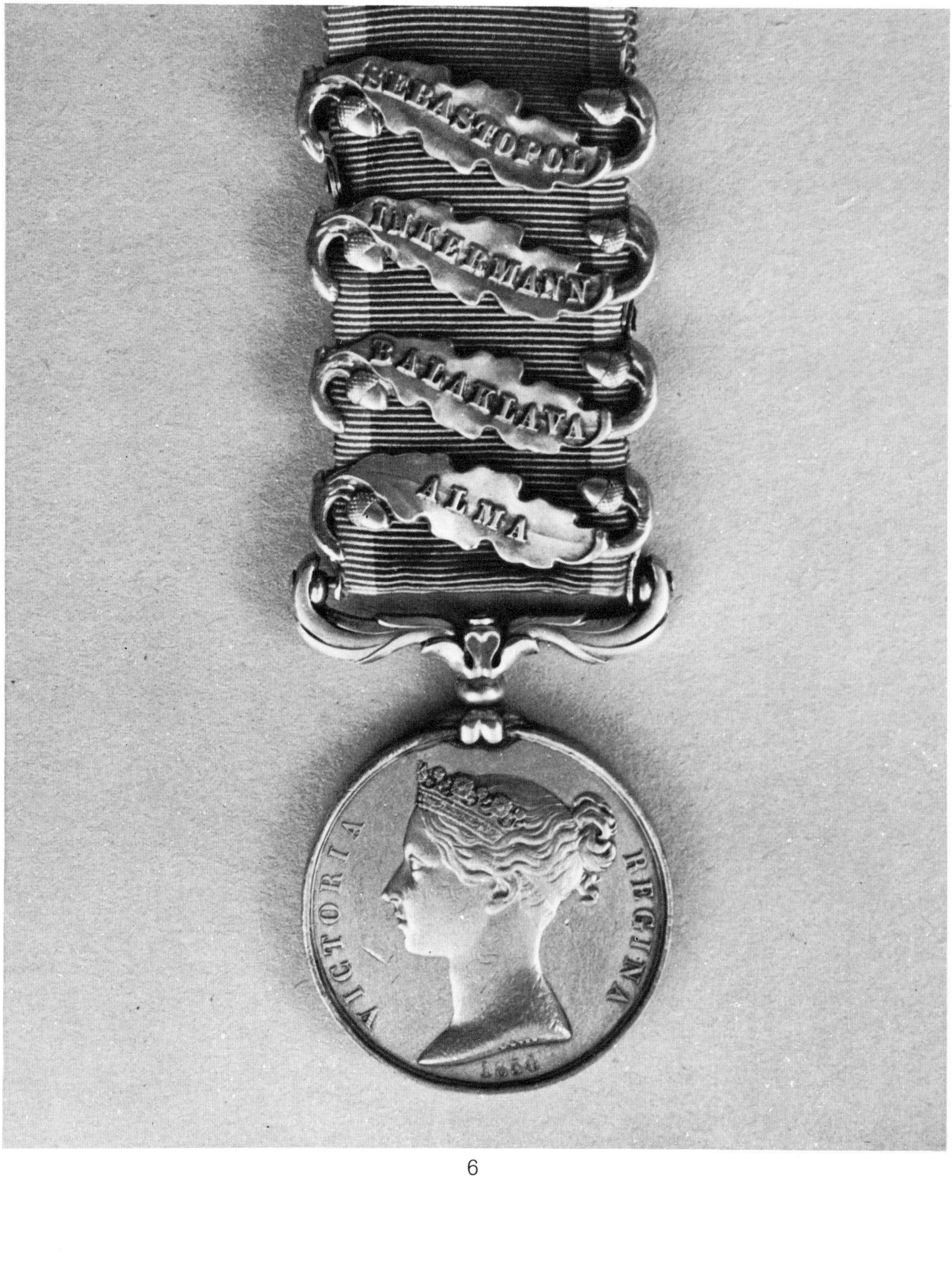
SEBASTOPOL
INKERMANN
BALAKLAVA
ALMA
VICTORIA REGINA

I. The Historical Background

Superficially, the settlement of the long Napoleonic interlude, at Vienna in 1814 and 1815, brought Europe nearly forty years of much-needed peace, which the Crimean War shattered. This apparent success can be attributed more to the war-weariness of Europe after Waterloo than to any inherent wisdom or virtue in the Vienna peace settlement. The arrangements to keep Europe quiet, with "legitimate" rulers and established boundaries, were influenced by the dominance of the largely reactionary Austrian minister, Count (later Prince) Metternich, and they therefore had sufficient strength and acceptance to withstand frequent pressure.

To appreciate the diplomatic manoeuvres of the period after 1815, it is best to view it as a struggle between old and new forces: the concept of Sovereign States wedded to the pursuit of power, inherited from the more or less benevolent despots of the eighteenth century; and the new ideas of Democracy and Nationalism guided by the concept of Liberty, unleashed after the French Revolution of 1789 though under a cloud in 1815. The sentiments associated with this "liberal revolution", though at first ascribed only to intellectuals, students and "subversive malcontents", were a perpetual, albeit latent, challenge to the established order, and were therefore systematically opposed. This was especially the case with traditionally autocratic or despotic states like Russia and Austria, which needed stability to preserve the privileged position of their ruling classes, and they tended to make common cause in "containing" the forces of change. (The leaders of Britain were apt to be broader and more practical in outlook, while France was not yet in a position to express an individual opinion.) While the Austro-Russian understanding lasted, the Vienna settlement prevailed, and no revolution, except that of Belgium in 1830, was successful.

The Crimea Medal was inscribed with the four major operations. It was worn proudly enough by those who had seen the job through. Yet when the medal was first issued, public feeling about the conduct of the war was such that ***Punch*** published a grim cartoon in which a near naked and frozen Guardsman, knee-deep in snow and threatened by vultures, tells his comrade that they are to have a medal – "Very kind," comes the reply, "Maybe one of these days we'll have a coat to stick it on!" (*National Army Museum.*)

Queen Victoria.

Signs of strain had been seen (1821-3) when Austrian troops had been used to quell a liberal insurrection in the Kingdom of Naples, in spite of a strong protest by Britain's Lord Castlereagh. However, a real rift developed after 1830. Mounting discontent in France, mainly over the Bourbon rulers restored in 1815, reached a climax in the July Revolution. Several other outbreaks occurred on the continent — "When France has a cold, all Europe sneezes—and in the consequent frenzy of diplomatic activity, a new alignment appeared between the liberal powers (Britain and France) and the autocracies. France remained a monarchy, under Louis-Philippe of the House of Orléans and, as the revolution was a compromise, no serious inroad had been made into the arrangements of 1815.

Concurrently, however, another problem was "hotting-up" for the Great Powers — not an internal one concerning authority and democracy, but an external one concerning their relations with a non-European power, that of the Sultan of Turkey. The Turks were losing their grip over the lands in south-east Europe that they had acquired, and the problem of who was to replace them occupied statesmen for most of the nineteenth century. Perhaps, with all its ramifications and rivalries, the "Eastern Question", as it was known, was the greatest international problem of the period, and the Crimean War an important milestone. Until the 1840s Russia had assumed the future of the Ottoman Empire was a matter to be determined between Turkey and herself, with or without agreement with Austria, her traditional ally. Thereafter it rapidly became a central issue in European politics. In the events leading up to the Crimean War one can begin to detect the considerations that were ultimately to divide Europe into two armed camps and lead to World War I.

These were the chief contenders.

Turkey

The Turks had advanced from their original Asiatic homeland into the Near East, capturing Constantinople in 1453. By cutting across the traditional trade routes they posed a problem for Europe that triggered off the Age of Overseas Discovery; they overran what is now known as the Balkan Peninsula, twice coming to the walls of Vienna and requiring the combined forces of Austria and Poland to halt them; their presence on the Mediterranean was an embarrassment to shipping. At its peak in mid-sixteenth century, under the Sultan Suleiman the Magnificent, this Muslim Ottoman Empire stretched from north Africa to the Caspian and from mid-Danube to the Indian Ocean. It was efficient, affluent, held Holy Cities and cultural centres, and it controlled Constantinople, which was the stepping-stone from Europe to Asia and which commanded the sea-route from the Aegean to the Black Sea.

As with so many empires success was not maintained, and by the eighteenth century the ebb had set in, with corruption in government, court intrigues, and military defeats by subject peoples. Always a redoubtable fighter, the Turk of the nineteenth century had lost his grip as an administrator. In view of the strategic position of the lands he occupied, his weakness and decline turned many envious eyes in his direction, and produced the nickname "Sick man of Europe". His presence in south-east Europe and his rule over Christian peoples seemed an anomaly and could easily be represented as a wrong that should be righted. His decline therefore created a marvellous opportunity for his neighbours, and others, to "fish in troubled waters". Until the 1850s Turkey had tended to be isolated diplomatically and had not enjoyed extensive support from the West, although France tended to be an ally. As recently as 1827 Turkey had faced a momentary combination of Britain, France and Russia and had suffered the loss of her fleet at Navarino.

Russia

Undoubtedly the chief source of pressure against the crumbling power of the Sultan came from the empire of the Czar. It adjoined Turkish territory to the north, it was vast in extent and manpower, and there were no popular institutions to check arbitrary or over-ambitious rulers. The Czar's sprawling domain was a colossus that could exert strong pressure. Alexander I, Czar from 1801 to 1825, had been weaned away from his earlier liberal attitudes by Metternich. Nicholas I, his younger brother who followed him and reigned until 1855, had likewise started by showing sympathy for domestic reforms; but, after having to suppress plots against his own position and a major uprising by the Poles in 1830, his attitude soon hardened into absolutism backed by military power. Autocratic and ambitious, and personally keen on military exploits, he concentrated on territorial expansion in Turkestan, Persia and the Caucasus, if only to pacify or forestall criticism at home against his repressive régime.

Turkey itself was central in his plans and ambitions, due to the lure of Constantinople and the attraction of ice-free ports in Asia Minor and the Aegean. (Russia's lack of ice-free ports has been one of the main influences on her foreign policy from Peter the Great until today.) She claimed a very special interest and role in the Sultan's Balkan lands on two other counts — religion and race. Hers was the largest country following the Orthodox Church, and furthermore the inhabitants of wide areas south of the Danube (Bulgars and Serbs especially) were the southern branch of the great Slav race.

The revolt of the Greeks against the Sultan in the 1820s had given the Czars an opportunity, but they did not exploit it whole-heartedly as they were not sympathetic to "revolutions from below". However, by the Treaty of Adrianople in 1829 and the guaranteeing of Greek independence in 1832, Russia made definite gains, e.g. more territory in the Caucasus, privileges for its merchants in Turkey, and a degree of protection over the principalities of Wallachia and Moldavia (now Rumania).

There followed further opportunities when Mehemet Ali, pasha of Egypt, attacked the Sultan's territory in Syria. This remarkable man, a most capable and ambitious ruler ably assisted by his son Ibrahim, had helped the Sultan against the Greeks, without receiving adequate reward. Outlawed by the Sultan, he overcame the Turkish forces in 1832. On an appeal by the Sultan to the powers, only Russia responded quickly; however the resulting peace which ceded Syria to Mehemet Ali was sufficiently humiliating to prompt the Sultan into a further understanding with an "obliging" Czar. The Treaty of Unkiar Skelessi in 1833 arranged for a military and naval alliance, with secret articles by which the Sultan undertook to close the Dardanelle Straits to the vessels of any other power. Russia was now achieving more by "friendship" and "adoption" than by force and opposition, and this period marks the peak of her success. Thereafter the problem of the Dardanelle Straits was recognised as a European concern and was regulated by the five powers. Russia accepted this arrangement as she hoped thereby to split the Anglo-French friendship.

Britain and France

Britain was rapidly establishing herself as the workshop of the world, and as the shipper and trader of the world; this ascendancy gave her tremendous importance and prestige which was reflected in her foreign policy under Palmerston. She often sympathised with movements of suppressed nationalities to achieve self-government, and at the same time kept a watchful eye on the expansion of rival powers, especially of Russia. Her policy was peaceful because war interfered with trade and damager her industrial production. An overriding belief in Free Trade was supported by commercial treaties. In contrast to all the hectic alarms and political excursions elsewhere in Europe, Britain was still a haven of calm and steady progress. She had already weathered the distress after 1815, and had started to put her house in order with a whole series of reforms in the 1830s — electoral, local government, factory and mines, poor law and public health; she was now endeavouring to find the answer to some of the unacceptable features of the new industrial age and the spirit of unfettered acquisitiveness that had marred its beginning. However the basic concern of the British government was to preserve the security of the Ottoman Empire, thereby ensuring the overland route to India, and preventing Russia from becoming a Mediterranean power. (The Congress of Vienna had made Britain a Mediterranean power, with Malta and a protectorate over Corfu and the Ionian Islands.)

France had sentimental and historical causes of interest in the Levant — a measure of traditional friendship with the Sultan, and since Napoleon's venture a commitment to Egypt in engineering and modernising Mehemet Ali's army. So France too was prepared to bolster up the Ottoman Empire, and was willing to work with Britain to check Russian influence and to keep the whole problem a concern for all the powers and not merely of any one. This partial identity of interest with Britain had been realised during Lord Palmerston's first spell as Foreign Minister in the early '30s, resulting in a joint protest to the Czar. Again in 1839, after the Sultan had tried unsuccessfully to reconquer Syria, the powers came together, and their mediation in the Convention of London, 1840, largely maintained the "status quo" — a disappointment to the Sultan, a check to further Russian designs, and also to France (with her cult for Mehemet Ali and her private desire for supremacy in the eastern Mediterranean). Louis-Philippe was neither diplomatically nor militarily strong enough to support Mehemet Ali in any further inroads into the Sultan's territory, and thereby suffered humiliation when a final settlement was reached without reference to him. However France was included in the Treaty of the Dardanelles, 1842, which closed the straits to the warships of all nations, so scrapping Unkiar Skelessi.

Domestic events in France at mid-century had a direct bearing on the developing international situation. Louis-Philippe abdicated early in 1848 after open insurrection in Paris. In spite of having the support of the middle classes who were profiting from the beginnings of the Industrial Revolution in France, he had steadily lost popular favour: the return of Napoleon's remains in 1840 had stirred memories of military glory; the new industrial methods were creating an urban proletariat turning towards socialist ideas; with Europe's mistrustful eye upon him he had followed an inglorious policy of non-participation and had been checked by Britain. To large numbers of Frenchmen, who in spite of 1815 knew themselves to be a leading intellectual and military force in Europe, the "bourgeois King" seemed identified with making France untrue to herself: it was no longer enough for him to parade his democratic attitude by gossiping with his subjects at the street-corner. After an altercation over the electoral system, he stood down and the Second Republic was established.

It looked at first as if this revolution in 1848, "the year of revolutions", was to succeed; but it quickly ran into trouble because of divided interests within (e.g. from intellectuals, socialists, Bonapartists, Bourbon legitimists) and panic after a short period of chaos caused France to look round for a "strong man". Louis Napoleon, nephew of the Emperor, emerged to form a "party of order" in the crisis. Elected president, he moved steadily towards personal rule, helped by army and police. His personal despotism was such that by the end of 1851 he had put an end to the Second Republic, and in December 1852 he took on the imperial title. So the Second Empire began, and the forces of liberal reform or revolution had a set-back.

Other important states *did* manage not to be involved in the Crimean confrontation, though their presence on the side-lines was not without influence. For a period after 1815 Austria under Count Metternich had been the dominant state on the continent, in general partnership with Russia. After 1848 and the Hungarian rising a certain "cooling off" in her relations with Russia appeared, as the Austrian empire comprised several branches of the Slav race, minorities subject to Vienna, which was bound to regard warily any extension of the Czar's influence in the adjacent Balkan Peninsula. Furthermore, Austria had been the traditional defender of Central Europe against the Turk, and geographical conditions (notably the course of the River Danube to the Black Sea) turned her attention eastward. Besides, she was not prepared to allow Russia to settle her scores with Turkey by herself and thereby to gain complete ascendancy in the Balkans and Asia Minor. So Austria was an "interested party" in the Eastern Question, but at this time was only active behind the scenes.

Prussia too, though a participant in most of the conferences and meetings, was not directly concerned in the events leading to actual warfare. Prussia was mainly interested in reaching a position of dominance among all the smaller German-speaking states, with a view to national unification. Austria, however, had been the traditional leader among the "small fry", and in 1850 Prussia was not quite ready for the eventual confrontation with the Vienna government.

The only other active participant was the small Kingdom of Piedmont or Sardinia, which offered its help to Britain and France, largely as a means of winning a place at the peace conference when it came — and thereby moving towards the unification of Italy under Piedmont's ruling house.

Thus, in the final count-down, Russia found herself without any allies over the Eastern Question, while Turkey was supported by Britain, France, Austria, Prussia and Piedmont.

* * * * * * * * *

The Black Sea.

2. The Crimean War

Towards Conflict

In the two years that preceded the actual outbreak of hostilities, certain ominous features can be seen. Britain's Foreign Minister, Lord Palmerston, was aiming to reduce Russian influence at Constantinople, and was succeeding. The ambassador, Sir Stratford Canning (Lord Stratford de Redcliffe), was one of the "old school" of diplomatists; a strong personality, who held a great sway over the Sultan. The Sultan was also disposed to listen to France, and his internal reforms, in matters like slave-markets and education, were making Turkey more acceptable to the west, and more inclined to follow a line independent of Russia. France's attitude was coming to be dominated by the ambition of Napoleon III, Emperor after 1852, whose unusual and unstable "romantic" character inclined him towards military ventures purely for prestige. The Czar, smarting under the loss of influence and equally disposed towards military exploits, saw an opportunity for interference in a somewhat unseemly squabble between the Greek and the Latin monks in the Holy Land (Turkish territory), over the guardianship of Christian Holy Places. By demanding equal privileges for Greek as for Latin monks, Nicholas used this "trumpery church-wardens' quarrel" to further his ambitions.

In 1844 and in early 1853 the Czar had attempted, by diplomatic means, to feel his way to an understanding with Britain on a "quid pro quo" basis, actually suggesting the dismemberment of the Sultan's lands — Russia to have a protectorate over Moldavia, Wallachia and Bulgaria, and Britain to take over Egypt and Crete. Even though morality does not appear to have weighed very heavily with any of the parties, this was turned down, because there was some sympathy in England for a reformed Turkey and much dislike of the autocratic Czar by people and government. When the Russian ambassador, Prince Menshikov, demanded equal treatment over the Holy Places and an acknowledgment of the Czar's protectorship over all the Sultan's Greek Christian subjects, the Sultan, on Lord Stratford's advice, agreed to the first point but refused the second. Diplomatic relations between Russia and Turkey were severed, and Menshikov left

The recruit. Height requirements on enlisting, if under twenty-five, were 5 ft 6½ in. to 5 ft 9 in. for heavy cavalry, 5 ft 6½ in. to 5 ft 8 in. for light cavalry, and a minimum of 5 ft. 5½ in. for infantry – and a little less if under nineteen. If these requirements make an interesting commentary on the standard physique of the time, so also do the payments made on enlisting – a so-called bounty of £5. 15s. 6d. for a cavalry recruit and £4 for an infantryman, of which sum most was for kit and necessaries, with 10s. for the recruit himself! (*Illustrated London News.*)

Constantinople; a Russian army advanced into and occupied Moldavia and Wallachia in spite of alarm among all the other powers and the exchange of protests and notes, including the Vienna Note sent jointly by Britain, France, Austria and Prussia. The Turks saw the infringement of their sovereignty as giving them no alternative, and in October 1853 they declared war against Russia. Public opinion in Britain had become increasingly enraged by Russia's aggrandisement policy, and it strongly pressed the government to take military measures, especially after Sinope when the Russians wiped out a Turkish flotilla. After further months of negotiations, the Central European powers declared their neutrality, but France and Britain agreed on armed intervention in support of Turkey, on 28 March, 1854.

Events in 1854

Operations against Russia in the Baltic were limited, as the Russian fleet avoided any confrontation with the British and French squadrons that entered the Gulf of Finland. Both in 1854 and again in 1855 bombardment of fortresses like Sveaborg and Kronstadt was

Preface to Reality. The Scots Guards cheer her Majesty before leaving for the Crimea.
The pre-embarkation parade, the "spit and polish" the cachet of Royalty present, this was the way that the Victorian would liked to have its war portrayed: the winter trenches before Sebastopol were yet to come. (*National Army Museum.*)

attempted, but lack of shallow-draught gunboats that could get in close to the island-fringed coast made it all of minor effectiveness, though the blockade was a blow to Russian trade and the presence of warships kept large Russian forces pinned down on shore.

In the Black Sea theatre of operations, French and British troops were sent in April and May to assist the Turkish forces which, during the winter, had put up an heroic resistance to the Russians along the lower Danube. The landings at Varna proved to be costly, but not on the battlefield. There was little activity, due to the skill of Omar Pasha and the quality of his Turkish troops, who halted the Russians, notably at Silistria, and caused their baffled retirement. The most deadly enemy proved to be cholera. Russian forces were withdrawn from Moldavia and Wallachia during the summer, but the western powers, having come thus far, were not returning without results. A joint expeditionary force of 25,000 British, under Lord Raglan, and 25,000 French, under Marshal St Arnaud, landed with 8,000 Turks on the west coast of the Crimean Peninsula on 14 September, establishing a beach-head about thirty miles north of their objective, the great Russian naval and military base of Sebastopol. This manoeuvre had proved easy as the Russian Black Sea fleet did not dispute their crossing but retired into the fine fortified harbour at Sebastopol and sank vessels across the entrance.

The Russians had shown dilatoriness at headquarters, where Count Paskevich, who did not take the Crimea threat seriously, was affronted by an appeal from Menshikov (now in command at Sebastopol) for reinforcements for his 25,000 man garrison. Not expecting a real assault so late in the season, Menshikov himself was taken by surprise, and though strengthened by the 16th Infantry Division, he took no action except "scorched earth" activity on the route of the invaders south to Sebastopol. This route took the allied force of nearly 60,000 men (with 128 guns but little cavalry) across the line of the small fordable Alma river. The British lacked horses and adequate supplies, while the Russians were handicapped by lack of proper staffwork and administration, and fell back on improvising defensive positions on the low hills which overlooked the Alma by a shallow cliff on its southern side. They neglected their extreme left flank where the hills ran out west to the sea in steep bluffs; and though, in the Battle of the Alma on 20 September, the British were twice repulsed before their superior rifle power gained the centre, the French on the right gained the heights more quickly and drove eastward to "roll up" the Russian positions.

Menshikov's outnumbered infantry lost over 5,000 men, against 2,000 British and about 1,000 French losses, the cavalry hardly entering into the few hours' engagement. With the Russians falling back on Sebastopol, the way should have been open for a quick follow-up. Although this was favoured by some of the field commanders (like General Cathcart of the British 4th Division), an unduly cautious, plodding approach was preferred by the elderly men in the allied high command who showed no sense of urgency.

Three days after the Alma, Menshikov moved the main body of his remaining forces north-east, apparently abandoning Sebastopol in order to keep open his rear communications with the Russian mainland through the narrow Perekop isthmus that was the only land link with the Crimea. The allies, with command of the sea, moved round to the south of Sebastopol and by 26 September were establishing themselves at new coastal bases, the British at Balaclava, the French at Kamiesh. This breathing space for the Russians was used with alacrity by Todleben, a military engineer officer whose genius was equalled only by his energy. Sebastopol's weakness — the land defences — were improved. To the east and south of the city, on the south side of the great harbour, he used the few remaining troops and sailors, helped by civilian labourers, to dig well-designed entrenchments and rifle-pits, and to throw up gigantic earthworks—all in about a fortnight. Menshikov moved back to Sebastopol at the beginning of October, steadily increasing the garrison. The war thus centred round a siege; this was to last eleven months and so was one of the longest in military history.

On 17 October the allies struck the first blow — a sea bombardment on a considerable scale (over 1,000 guns), but it proved unproductive. Menshikov, powerfully reinforced by hussars and cossacks as well as three infantry divisions, replied on the 25th with a move towards the British base-port of Balaclava, starting the famous battle of that name.

The Russians drew first blood by capturing four redoubts despite a spirited resistance by their Turkish defenders. However a cavalry detachment moving towards Kadikoi on the road to Balaclava was held by Highland infantry in the "Thin Red Line"; the main body of the advancing Russian cavalry was dispersed in a stirring charge by Scarlett's Heavy Brigade of Cavalry. Lord Raglan was anxious to avoid losses in his limited cavalry strength, but when it appeared that the Russians were going to remove guns from the captured redoubts, he sent a belated and hasty note to General Lucan in command of the Cavalry Division to advance and engage the Russians manning the guns. The guns in question were in "dead ground" to Lucan in the valley. (At this period there were no precise map references pin-pointing objectives.)

Failing to glean any further enlightenment from the impetuous Captain Nolan who brought the order, the Light Brigade, led by the gallant but disdainful Lord Cardigan, launched themselves without infantry or artillery support for the better part of two miles to Liprandi's Russian gunners at the far end of the valley. They sabred the gunners but, harried by cossacks, were unable to move the guns and had no alternative but to return — less than 200 of the 700 who had set out. The French were largely distant spectators, aghast at the suicidal venture, and General Bosquet's famous remark, "C'est magnifique, mais ce n'est pas la guerre", was extremely apt.

The next engagement — the Battle of Inkerman on 5 November — came quickly. Menshikov, under strong pressure from the Czar, decided on an ambitious plan that involved over forty battalions in a surprise attack, partly under cover of darkness, on the British positions on the heights east and south-east of Sebastopol. It involved an approach from two directions and, with subsidiary diversionary sorties, called for perfect timing. Disagreement among the inadequately briefed field commanders, coupled with poor visibility and difficult map-reading, played havoc with the Russian plan. The force of 8,000 British near Inkerman, taken unawares and short of ammunition, maintained their position with great valour against their confused attackers who outnumbered them many times over; and after some hours of hand-to-hand fighting the arrival of some French reserve troops under General Bosquet clinched the encounter. Russian casualties exceeded 11,000 (including six generals), against 4,500 by the allies. Once more Menshikov was forced back behind the Sebastopol defences.

A few days after, on 14 and 15 November, the late autumn storms, which were typical of the Crimea, wrought havoc not only among the (inadequately) encamped British on the exposed ground around Balaclava, but also among the supply ships in the narrow over-crowded harbour. Immense amounts of food and materials, medical supplies and ships themselves were destroyed or rendered useless. The country roads became almost unusable, and movement of any sort extremely harassing. Only one further problem was likely to occur, and it did — the Russian cold!

Some Repercussions

The situation had not gone un-noticed in London: *The Times* was reporting the trials as well as the triumphs. William Howard Russell had joined the staff of the paper ten years before as a young man in his twenties. He went to the Crimea at the outbreak of hostilities and stayed throughout, the first of the great "special correspondents". A series of letters and reports — not at first acceptable or popular reading — opened the public's eyes to the sufferings of British troops, raised questions as to the adequacy of preparations and supplies, and finally revealed a measure of mismanagement and incompetence that discredited Lord Aberdeen's ministry, which fell in February, 1855.

A Medical Corps without proper supplies or even huts for field hospitals was not in a position to do its work, and early in the campaign news of the suffering and appalling death-roll among the over-crowded casualties at the base hospital at Scutari, on the Bosphorus opposite Constantinople, reached the ears of Florence Nightingale. This lady's genteel upbringing had not prevented her from visiting hospitals all over Europe in her desire to learn, and she herself trained as a nurse. When, in September, 1854, the wounded from the Alma added to the hundreds dying from sickness, she offered to organise a nursing service at Scutari, and left on 21 October with thirty-four nurses. She arrived just in time to receive the Inkerman casualties, who swelled the total to 10,000 men in her care. Ascribing the appalling mortality to bad sanitary conditions, she found that her struggle was not only against sickness and poor facilities and treatment, but also against officialdom and "red tape". She has been accused of an impatient and autocratic attitude, but tough situations demanded tough remedies, and growing publicity and public opinion were on her side, and her work transformed military hospital procedure. Her devotion to the sick and wounded was unwavering. She achieved order out of chaos at Scutari, and organised (though she did not actually run) three hospitals in the Crimea itself. Though affected by fever herself, she kept going in her work at Scutari and only stopped when the British left in July, 1856.

Until 1855 the British had incurred the largest and most costly part of the operation; thereafter the French tended to play the major part. This was partly the result of the way Russian tactics in the later stages happened to involve the French, and partly through a tacit understanding among the allies that the British were no longer in a state to bear the burden. It was not a question of morale, but of decreased effectiveness caused by battle losses, by the overwork, strain and sheer misery of life in the winter of 1854-5 when supplies of everything were short, and by the unforseen high sickness rate. (At one point the 63rd regiment was reduced to ninety-three men.) Thoughts of peace were frequently voiced, but never undermined a dogged determination to survive and "see it through".

Events in 1855

Winter had brought an end to set-piece battles, but conditions were such as to strain the best troops. The siege dragged on, as units of the allies kept unceasing watch on the great fortress and arsenal (now well-manned) from which the Russians would make occasional probing sallies. (Sebastopol's land communication with mainland Russia was kept open by road across the Crimea and through the Perekop isthmus). Rain, snow and frost made movement a nightmare, and the supply position had not improved enough to make existence more than just tolerable either at base or in the trenches. The Russians were in little better plight. Both sides would occasionally attempt under cover of darkness to improve their position or their field of fire by establishing rifle-pits, advance posts or further forward trenches, so that the area of no-man's-land tended steadily to shrink.

January saw the official entry into the war of the Kingdom of Piedmont or Sardinia on the side of the allies, but it was mid-May before the 15,000 infantry contingent actually landed and saw action. In February the numerically stronger French agreed to take over responsibility for the formidable Malakhov fortifications, leaving the British to oppose the smaller Redan from their sector. But Russian cannonballs and shells from several other points along their defence-line continued to make life unpleasant, and though casualties only numbered one or two at a time, a witness wrote with horror of the numbers of cairns and crosses which soon began to appear at every camp-site.

The death of Czar Nicholas early in March heralded changes in the Russian high command. Menshikov was removed to make way for General Count Osten-Sacken in command of the Sebastopol garrison, and Prince Michael Gorchakov of the Crimea in general. On 10 March the Russians advanced and occupied the Mamelon, a hillock in front of the Malakhov bastion; their Great Night Sortie twelve days later to push the French further back proved a costly failure. For a time there were rumours of peace negotiations — and it is significant that during the truce that followed the Sortie there was much fraternising between Russians and allies. (A conference did in fact meet in Vienna on 15 March, and though abortive it lasted till June.)

With the coming of better weather, operations of a more positive nature could have been expected. British infantry now totalled some 16,000 men in good health, and a fair hospital service was working. The supply position too had improved with the completion of a seven-mile rail link, initially worked by horses, between the wharves at Balaclava and the British lines up on the high ground.

A heavy bombardment on 9 April was not followed up by any general assault, and though the Italian ally provided useful reinforcements in May, the next venture — to deny the Russians the unimpeded use of the Sea of Azov — was a seaborne expedition east along the Crimea coast to the Strait of Kerch. The first attempt on 4 May was abandoned, but the second later in the month gained Kerch, Yenikale and Anapa for the allies.

On land, however, developments were slow, though among the armies, as the peace hopes of March faded, word got around that "something was afoot". In view of this tendency for the siege to continue seemingly endlessly, it may be worth while to draw attention to the general character of the contestants, remembering how commentators, contemporary and historical, have sought to apportion blame.

The Armies

Owing to commitments in India and elsewhere, this was not Britain's "First Eleven"; their numbers were sadly eroded by sickness and casualties, yet they maintained something of the "Agincourt spirit" in standing their ground, and their doggedness in the face of unforeseen hardships was admirable. Their officers too have been criticised: their letters and diaries sometimes give the impression that they were amateurs hoping to play a gentlemanly part in a military game. Their tendency to under-rate the Russian peasant troops, their concern for promotion and advancement, and over "who was dining with whom", can be discounted in the face of battle casualties and the roll of honour which proved their courage and competence in the field. The High Command cannot escape some measure of censure, though Lord Raglan, an ageing Commander-in-Chief who had been a fine soldier but was cast for this most exacting post when most men would be enjoying retirement, can be cleared of many of the charges commonly brought. The prime factors responsible for the British failure to cut short a dragging campaign were the crippling losses of medicines, tents, food and arms in the destructive storms of November, the examples of dilatoriness and error on the part of headquarters in despatching further supplies, and the fact that Britain entered the war without proper preparation. Distance from Britain and difficulty over quick communication were a problem for the administrative side of the army, which had been allowed to run down for thirty years. Sickness and disease on a massive scale had not been foreseen, and the winter weather of the Crimea, in spite of its sheltered south-east coast, not anticipated.

The French too had their troubles. Just as Menshikov was subject to interference by Czar Nicholas, so the French High Command — first St Arnaud and then Generals Canrobert and Bosquet — had to defer to the orders and advice of Emperor Napoleon III, who at one point intended to appear in person and command operations. In spite of the inevitable jibes from the British about the drunkenness and disorderliness of their French counterparts, and their aptitude for looting, there was also plenty of good comradeship, and the French commanders (better supplied and with easier access to their coastal base than the British above Balaclava) were often accommodating over food, horses and ambulances. On the whole there was perhaps a greater "professionalism" on the part of French officers and commanders, and a greater "élan" than the stolid British showed.

The Turks, who had shown themselves such doughty fighters in the early months when they had faced the Russians alone along the Danube, did not figure so prominently in the Sebastopol siege. Many had been sent to harass the Russians in the Caucasus and Circassia to the east of the Black Sea.

As for the Russians, their tenacity in the face of hardship and danger must be acknowledged. "Ivan" was generally a serf, and commonly pitied or despised as such. Unschooled and unused to thinking, military service was an obligation that only good fortune could enable him to avoid, but for which his origins as a countryman used to "roughing it" were a good preparation. Discipline was strict and harsh. The poor pay and food which he received as a soldier was only a continuation of everyday experience for one who lived on rye-bread, cabbage soup and buckwheat porridge. He was physically tough, dogged in spirit, and with an immense fatalistic capacity for dumb suffering. Most of the Crimean troops had walked, marched or shuffled all the 800 miles from Central Russia to Sebastopol, as commandeered carts and their drivers were not allowed to pass beyond their home regional boundary. The lot of the Russian soldier, like that of his British counterpart, was not improved by the inefficiency and downright corruption of headquarters in St Petersburg or Moscow: the main supply route to the south was said to be marked by a line of graves, abandoned equipment and dead horses.

The Finale

In June, activity increased. The Third Bombardment opened up on the afternoon of the 6th and continued into the 7th, over 500 guns silencing the Mamelon and other Russian batteries. Two French divisions successfully attacked the Volhynia and Selenginsk Redoubts; and two other divisions, the Mamelon. The latter were counter-attacked but a regrouping under General Bosquet finally occupied and held the position, while detachments from the British 2nd and Light Divisions stormed the Quarries—trenches in front of the Redan opposite the British sector. French losses were over 5,000, British over 600, of whom 47 were officers. This had been planned as the first round in the final assault on Sebastopol, but it was followed by failure and disillusionment.

The day chosen was 18 June — the anniversary of Waterloo. On the previous day a strong bombardment had apparently silenced the Redan batteries, but their silence was a ruse. Early next morning, the French were to have attacked the Malakhov and the British the Redan after further artillery preparation; but the French attack began prematurely and upset the time-table. Lord Raglan certainly blundered in sending a few hundred men without artillery support to attack the Redan, and both the allies suffered terribly from broadsides from Russian warships in Sebastopol harbour and from naval guns brought ashore from scuttled vessels. Confusion followed as field officers found themselves cut off from central direction and having to improvise. By 8 a.m. it was all over, the only gain being a small stretch of ground, the Cemetery. French losses were 3,500, British 1,500, as against the Russians 1,500 (and 4,000 during the previous day's bombardment). The causes of failure were the lack of central planning, the political pressure on General Pélissier to change his plans over timing, and the withdrawal of General Bosquet from command of the assault.

Lord Raglan died a few days after and this held up proceedings until General Simpson had been installed as the new Commander in Chief. The French were receiving reinforcements and it was the Emperor's wish that these should be used to draw out the Russians into the open. General Pélissier however was determined that the siege must not be allowed to last into another winter. His success in this direction was perhaps helped by an ill-advised Russian venture in mid-August. Against his better judgment, but urged by the new Czar, Alexander II, Gorchakov attacked the French (who were supported by a few Sardinians and Turks) along the Chernaya River. After heavy fighting the Russians were repulsed with 8,000 casualties

Arms and equipment identify these men as the Durham Light Infantry and not, as might be supposed, as Russian volunteers from the steppes of Siberia or Mongolia! Queen's Regulations are silent about wearing coats of sheepskin (on the left)or goatskin (the bugler, with one cross-belt), or of deerstalker and sou'wester headgear, or of varied boots! *(National Army Museum.)*

(including eleven generals and 250 officers) — a loss which must severely have reduced their chances of final success.

The allies almost immediately began to press hard the disconcerted defenders, by sapping and mining, making further advance trenches, and until 8 September by an almost ceaseless bombardment. The end came suddenly and quickly, and though the statement might have seemed ironic and callous to the appalling list of casualties on that day — 10,000 allies and 13,000 Russians—there was an element of anti-climax. Despite another British failure to take the Redan, the French overwhelmed the Malakov in quarter of an hour — after months of effort! Its fall left the approach to the town, arsenal and docks wide open; Gorchakov was convinced that further defence was pointless, and in one night, by means of a bridge of boats and any small vessels available, evacuated the whole of the surviving garrison and abandoned the city and its installations to fire and demolition. The allied troops entered on the morning of 9 September and found their erstwhile enemies well away on the north side of the great estuary. No attempt was made to follow up and pursue, so the Crimean struggle came to an end at the same halting, "stop-go" tempo on which it had begun.

3. Reflections and Results

With the end of the siege, hostilities had virtually finished, apart from some skirmishing along the Black Sea coast and a few "face saving" Russian successes against the Turks in the Caucasus. This tiresome struggle may almost be said to have "fizzled out". It was March, 1956, before a treaty of peace was signed at Paris. By its provisions, the Czar had to renounce all claims to protecting the Sultan's Christian subjects and to territory in Moldavia and Wallachia; the Black Sea was neutralised, Russian warships and arsenals being forbidden, and the Sultan's empire placed under a guarantee of the Great Powers.

However, though Russia had to submit to these terms as loser, it is yet possible to assert that there was no real winner of the Crimean War: it has great importance in the general stream of historical development, but the "profit and loss account" of the contestants showed a variable picture, and some of the Paris peace arrangements had little strength or permanence. Even Russia the loser was able to repudiate the de-militarization of the Black Sea after only a few years, and to have designs on detaching Bessarabia from Moldavia. Turkey had been confirmed in its control of Constantinople, but in a very short time the whole question of Turkish control of part of Europe was to be re-opened.

France perhaps came off best among the victors: there was a fair measure of military glory to wipe out the memory of Waterloo, the Second Empire of Emperor Napoleon III had re-asserted its position as a leading Great Power, and the Emperor was able to "play host" at the peace conference. His ambitions, sustained by an improved economy at home and (for a few years at least) by popular support, found expression in a brilliant court life of banquets and social or diplomatic gatherings; but even this "success story" was transient: the reckoning was soon to come, as the events of the 1860s and 1871 were to show.

A group at headquarters. The doorway frames Lord Raglan (in civilian clothes) and Marshall Pélisser, the British and French Commanders in Chief, with attendant Staff and Aides, (including a Spahi). Lord Raglan's death occurred a few days after the taking of this photograph. (*National Army Museum.*)

Britain's legacy from the war and the Paris peace treaty was not really substantial. The overland route to India was secured by keeping the Russians out of Constantinople, but the necessity for this was soon to be diminished when the opening of the Suez Canal at the end of the next decade provided a more congenial alternative by sea. Britain's place in the Mediterranean was in any case sufficiently asserted through Gibraltar and Malta; and in little more than twenty years, Cyprus and a preponderating influence in Egypt had been acquired — in spite of Britain's moral gesture in refusing to join Czar Nicholas in dismembering Turkey in the early 1850s. Some of the most far-reaching effects of the Crimean War were to be seen in the widespread reforms in the administration of the British army and in the arrangement of medical services. This latter reform was based on the recommendations of Florence Nightingale who had done such invaluable work in the Crimea during the war. To bystanders in Europe the lesson was not lost that Britain did not always provide a Marlborough or a Wellington to direct its ventures and that its army had been so ill prepared at the outbreak of war.

There was one bystander in particular to whom this revelation was of great interest: Prussia had taken no active part in the hostilities, but was certainly concerned with the outcome. The Prussian military and diplomatic leaders, including Bismarck, were of the opinion that Britain could be "written off" as a military force on the continent.

The importance of the Crimean War was that it was the first great check to Russia's imperial advance; loss of prestige gave a setback to absolutist rule in Russia itself and prepared the way for criticism and some internal reforms. Further, the "peace" of Europe under the iron hand of the Czar in league with equally absolutist Austria no longer persisted: Russia was furious over Austria's neutrality. The latter had not openly taken either side, but her action in occupying parts of the Balkans was considered an unfriendly act, and it opened up a possible area of disagreement and rivalry between the two autocratic powers. A colossus had fallen in Europe, and in so doing had made a breach through which a third party found it easier to reach towards leadership and pre-eminence on the continent. This third party was not France, momentarily enjoying the euphoria of victory, but Prussia, aspiring to lead other German states into united nationhood and strengthened by the setback to the understanding between Russia and Austria. Thereafter European relations were to pivot round Prussia rather than the Russo-Austrian axis of the previous half century.

Another important result was that the final collapse and partition of the Ottoman Empire was postponed for over another sixty years, and the five powers agreed collectively to guarantee its independence and integrity. The neutrality of the Black Sea was also ensured for the immediate future, and Russia's designs to expand westward were temporarily curbed.

There were other side effects of the Crimean War, notably the way Prime Minister Cavour of the Kingdom of Piedmont was able to use the diplomatic meetings to keep a "united Italy" question in the public eye. ("You have the future of Italy in your haversacks", he had told his troops embarking for the Crimea, and they had fought well, albeit belatedly, to earn a place at the conference table.) But these other results of the war were of secondary significance compared with the way that Britain was tending to withdraw from Europe, while Prussia was preparing to enter more strongly into the military-diplomatic game and all the five main contestants were re-appraising their policies and alignments. In the game of power politics there is little room for sentiment. Friends and allies are courted or discarded according to the expediency of the moment, and there was going to be more than one change round before the final showdown in 1914, in spite of the long discernible tendency of the Central Europeans to keep together. So the Crimea is chiefly significant in concluding one chapter in European rivalries and starting another. Indeed some historians refer to it as "a milestone on the road to Armageddon".

It is sometimes said that this "milestone" could have been avoided and Europe thereby diverted on to a different road forward. Even if one tries to apportion blame or responsibility, the Crimean War provides more debatable points than certainties, more questions than answers. Czar Nicholas and his ambitions must be given high priority on the list of those responsible, but was war the only possible answer to him? Could Austria, with her "special relationship" with Russia, have achieved something by taking a more positive stance early on? Were Britain and France wise in the extent to which they bolstered up an admittedly "sick man" in a condition that could not long be maintained? Could blame be attached to Sir Stratford Canning, British ambassador at Constantinople, for following what appears to be a strong personal line? Or must the French Emperor be made the arch-villain of the whole business deluding himself and trying to delude others with his dreams of military might and glory? (The traveller and writer A. W. Kinglake certainly thought so, and, after going to the Crimea in 1854, his eight-volume history of the campaign was so bitingly critical of Louis-Napoleon that it was banned in France for a life time!) Perhaps however his judgment, if report speaks true, was not unbiased.

A purely British viewpoint of the Crimean venture must inevitably be tinged with regrets. From the moment British troops disembarked at Varna bad luck, bad management, hesitant leadership and disease had dogged their progress. Justifiably or not, they felt that they had a worthy job to do — to oppose a tyrant — and that the prevailing conditions denied them the chance of even reasonable military honours in performing it. Disease turned out to be a worse enemy. The sick and wounded were sent back mainly to Scutari, but some went for treatment or convalescence to Malta which had figured as a port of call, supply depot and mustering point for men and material bound for the Crimea; its military hospital of Mtarfa grew in importance as the century progressed. The more discerning observer today, viewing the burial ground in a quiet spot below the nearby ramparts and learning of the invalids from India and Africa who had followed those from the Crimea, may well meditate soberly on the price of Empire and overseas military ventures.

* * * * * * * * *

Embarkation

EMBARKATION OF THE 11TH HUSSARS, AT KINGSTOWN.

THE busy scene engraved upon the next page is one of the many Illustrations which the Services now present of the movements towards the seat of the War. Here we have the Embarkation, on the 15th ult., of a portion of the 11th Hussars, on board the troop-ship *Tyrone*, in Kingstown harbour. This splendid vessel, which was built last autumn, at Bathurst, is 1197 tons register, and carries the pennant of Lieut. Raymond, R.N.; has been chartered by Government for four months certain, and eight or twelve, if required to convey troops to the East. This fine vessel is fitted up for 60 horses in the lower hold, 70 men between decks, and 6 officers in the poop cabin. She had on board—54 horses, 62 men, and 5 officers. Of infantry, she accommodates 600 troops and 25 officers. The men were in high spirits, and fraternised with the sailors admirably; all joining at the evening twilight in singing, in very good style, "Annie Laurie," "Auld Lang Syne," and other favourite songs. There are on the main-deck four 18-pound guns; each of the crew, fifty in number, is furnished with a musket and bayonet; and there is also on board an ample supply of cutlasses, pikes, pistols, and ammunition. Thus armed, and taking into consideration the number of soldiers also on board, there was little fear of anything untoward occurring to the noble ship or her gallant freight from attacks. Her great speed is another security. On her passage from Liverpool to Dublin, with but a light wind, she sailed at the rate of $10\frac{1}{2}$ knots per hour, close hauled; and she has attained the rate of 15 knots, or nautical miles, per hour, running free. This gives us hope that it will not be long before we hear of the gallant 11th being safely landed in the East.

Embarkation of the 11th Hussars, at Kingstown. At the start of hostilities, contemporary accounts would speak re-assuringly of embarkation – the speed of new vessels chartered by the government, their armament, the well-armed crews, the accommodation for hundreds of men and dozens of horses, the high morale. The ***Tyrone,*** shown here, is taking on part of the Light Brigade. It was to prove anything but a "tidy" war, when distance, weather, inefficiency and human error lent a hand. (*Illustrated London News.*)

Left: The original *Illustrated London News* caption to the engraving above.

French troops, undeterred by the primitive gangway, embark in light-hearted mood on their transport for Turkey and the Crimea. The Emperor Napoleon's men, though inevitably criticised by their British allies for being slack in a military sense, were keen to prove themselves and assert their country's traditional place of honour among the armies of Europe.
(*Illustrated London News.*)

Right: Emperor Napoleon III. The personal character of rulers undoubtedly contributed towards the tragedy of the Crimean War. The ambitious policies of the Czar had resulted in a "war situation", and the effect of the French Emperor was to "fan the flames". Personally ambitious, the dubious means by which he had assumed royal power necessitated his following a policy that increased French prestige. He was interested in military exploits, and was given to interfering with the conduct of the war by his generals; but he lacked the flair of his great uncle.

Encampment of the Rifle Brigade at Constantinople – from a Daguerreotype by J. Robertson.

The "James Robertson" responsible for the daguerreotypes from which these prints were made was chief engraver at the Imperial Mint at Constantinople. A keen photographer, modern photography would have given him wonderful scope for the arrival and establishment (at Scutari and Gallipolli, and later at Varna) of the first units of the Expeditionary Force in a near-eastern setting. At that time, no shot had been fired in anger, and the general impression conveyed is one of cool confidence, with everything in order – even the off-duty infantry at their "chores". If further re-assurance was needed for the folks back at home, then the long orderly lines of infantry tents, the distinctive uniform of the Rifle Brigade and the very presence of the Foot Guards supplied it! (*Both engravings Illustrated London News.*)

H.B.M. Foot Guards at Scutari – from a Daguerreotype by Mr. Robertson, of Constantinople.

Above: British infantry in barracks at Gallipoli. (*Illustrated London News.*)

Below: Officers' quarters at Scutari. Situated across the Bosphorus from Constantinople, Scutari meant different things to different people. It had relatively spacious encampments on terra firma for newly arrived troops, in Mediterranean sunshine and semi-oriental surroundings. The officers' quarters were in airy, high-ceilinged rooms in the barracks which the Sultan made available. Scutari also meant a more or less clean bed for the wounded or the cholera victim, provided that delays in crowded transports and waiting in corridors had not already proved fatal. (*Illustrated London News.*)

Balaclava harbour

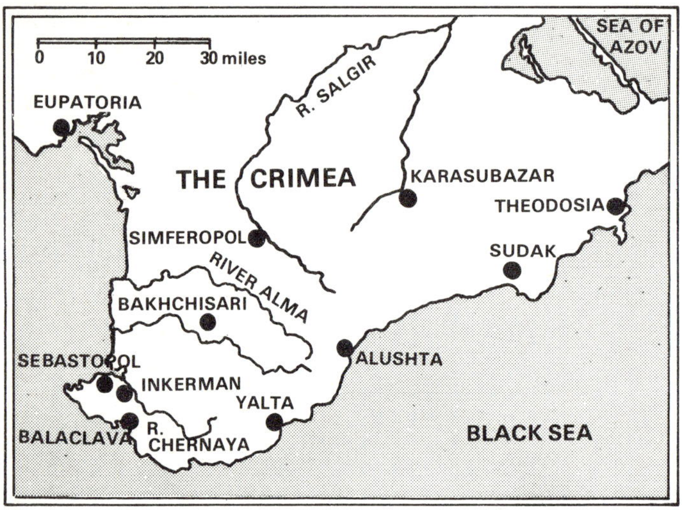

Above: Balaclava Harbour. The little settlement beside the narrow sheltered inlet, flanked by steep rocky slopes and guarded by the ruins of an old Genoese fort, became the British base. Access to the upland, across which ran the route to Sebastopol, was by a difficult narrow track, which had to be negotiated by wagons; later seven miles of rail were constructed. There was little room for easy movement, and the small harbour was very congested. The storms of mid-November 1854, with hurricane-force winds, created great havoc and destruction among the shipping, and the appalling loss of food, medicines and supplies in general resulted in hardship for the troops all winter. (*Ron Harris.*)

Left: Map of the Crimea.

Right: Seamen from a British Man O'War drawn from life by George Thomas. (*Illustrated London News.*)

Above left: "Roughrider" Macnamara of the 5th Dragoon Guards.

Left: Colour-Sergeant Macgregor. The Scots Guards Colour Sergeant's insignia are clear, as are the shoulder-sash, the buttons in threes (they were the 3rd Regiment of Foot Guards), the magnificent bearskin and the Crimean War medal.

Above right: Three tough Crimean veterans of the Coldstream Guards. Their beards were allowed during the Crimean winter. Note the heavy packs, with mess tin in its waterproof cover strapped on the blanket. They lean their arms on a heavy wooden water bottle.

Right: Private in Full Marching Order. His foot regiment is the 28th, the North Gloucesters, which figured at the Alma and Inkerman, and in the siege.
(*All pictures National Army Museum.*)

British infantry Corporal (left) and officer. They are in the uniforms worn at the Alma—virtually full dress. Officers and soldiers usually rid themselves of their hard shakos at the first opportunity, replacing them with soft forage caps.

The British regiments wore a wide variety of uniform. The line infantry regiments could be distinguished from each other by the colour of cuffs and collars, the patterns on the white tape on their coats and regimental badges and belt plates. Riflemen wore very dark green uniforms; artillery blue with red cuffs and collars; highlanders wore kilts. There were many minor variations in dress peculiar to certain regiments. The harsh conditions in the Crimea soon produced a strangely clad arming which wore anything which would keep the cold out—including civilian clothes.

British Private and Sergeant. Both wear the dark grey overcoats and forage caps which were typical of the British infantry as the weather grew colder. When the snows came even these uniform garments disappeared under almost anything that could be found.

Above left: N.C.O.s and Men of the 68th, the famous Durham Light Infantry, which won Crimean battle honours at the Alma, Inkerman and Sebastopol. At the Alma, which followed quickly after the initial September landing, the men marched into battle in full regimentals – scarlet coats with green (or blue, yellow or buff) facings. But winter did not allow the troops to appear so well turned-out as the men in the photograph!

Below left: Officers and Other Ranks of an Infantry Regiment. The variety of uniform and the simple act of piling arms help to give point to this well-posed group, both historically and photographically. The lance-corporal in forage cap, great-coat and cape appears well protected. The two officers, at their ease in shell jackets (one with the new gold shoulder cords) and undress caps, contrast with the three privates in full-dress coatees and dress shakos. Apparently all have white facings, which suggests the 41st (Welsh) Regiment.

Above: Captain Henry Duberly and Mrs. Duberly. The Crimean War abounded in minor curious and incongruous features, many of which, it must be admitted, stemmed from the fact that British officers for the most part were members of the "upper classes," and naturally, as far as conditions allowed, carried on as usual! It took more than Russian troops and Russian weather to prevent an occasional hunt or race-meeting; there were "T.G.s" (travelling gentlemen) who "looked in" at the Crimea with a pass to stroll through the trenches; and the presence of officers' wives at the front was not unknown – hence the dashing Mrs. Duberly!
(All three pictures National Army Museum.)

Lieutenant of French line infantry regiment, fusileer company. In the background is a Zouave of the 3rd. Regiment. The French uniforms were smart and impressive. Many nations, notably the Americans, Italians and British, copied French styles. Even the Russians adopted some of the French styles after the Crimean War.

French discipline was slack by British standards but their army was more experienced and professional than the British. The officer wears a gold laced kepi and a caban coat, the sleeves richly decorated with gold lace. The Zouaves wore Arabian style uniforms although they were composed of Europeans. The distinctive uniforms and excellent fighting record made the Zouaves an élite part of the French army.

Corporal, French Foreign Legion, in the trenches around Sebastopol, 1854-55. The Legion suffered badly from cholera, losing 200 men including two regimental commanders. They fought at the Alma and at Inkerman but they gained great renown for their bravery during the siege of Sebastopol.

The Corporal wears the same basic uniform as the rest of the French infantry. This included a "kepi", a "capote" (overcoat), and red trousers tucked into long, once-white gaiters. He carries a bayonet and a short sword called a "coup-choux".

WINTER DRESS FOR THE TROOPS IN THE CRIMEA.

To protect our troops from the rigour of the Crimean winter, a variety of new provision has been made in the clothing, with almost unexampled rapidity. We have engraved specimens of these new dresses. The head-dress, or cap, is composed of sealskin, shaped after the fashion of those worn by the Arctic Region explorers, and made to be almost round the entire head. The cap to be worn by the officers is composed of fine brown fur, "helmet shape," and lined with brown silk. A large flap falls under the back of the neck and under the chin, so that very little of the face is exposed. The cap to be worn by the private is of the same shape, less refined, though as strong in texture. The cap has been pronounced by several officers and non-commissioned officers to be an article which combines warmth with ease. The officer's coat, or cloak, is made in the military style, and is composed of richly-finished fur, brown in colour. The coat for the non-commissioned officers and men is of a somewhat different shape and texture, and will, unlike that of the officers, have a waterproof shoulder-covering.

Officers and men will alike wear very strong overalls, to be composed of cow-hide. Of these, Messrs. Almond and Co., of St. James's-street, have supplied no fewer than 44,000 suits for the men, and 10,000 suits for the officers. They also forward a proportionate quantity of under-clothing, and close upon 50,000 gauntlets, or large gloves, composed of fur. We may confidently anticipate the winter clothing will be a great boon to our gallant troops.

The quantity of stores which have been sent from the Tower is astonishing. Amongst other things, a short time since, 90,000 pairs of the best lamb's wool drawers, 200,000 pairs of gloves, 200,000 pairs of stockings of the best lamb's wool, 50,000 morning-gowns for the hospitals, lined throughout with flannel, and 30,000 great-coats, to be used over those worn on ordinary occasions, when on guard or on picket, were shipped in one day.

Above: Winter dress for the Crimea. When the authorities had realized that Crimean cold and wind were as hostile as Russian troops, they despatched large quantities of approved new items of clothing, basing their design upon the experience of Arctic explorers. All shades of home opinion were re-assured by contemporary prints and accounts which emphasized the richly-finished fur and silk lining of officers' coats and caps, while other ranks had "less refined" garments, "though as strong in texture." (*Illustrated London News.*)

Left: The original caption for the above engraving.

Right: Officers of the "Black Watch". Their apparel shows varying degrees of adaptation to a Crimean winter! Except for his peaked forage cap the officer at the left of the picture is in full dress with crimson sash, ornamental dirk at his waist, goatskin sporran and broadsword. The officer next to him wears a truly fantastic costume of tartan suit, light waistcoat, forage cap, bow tie and sea boots. The other two officers are more typical, in forage caps, "Crimea" jackets and tartan trousers. (*National Army Museum.*)

Left: Company officer of a Russian Grenadier Regiment. This officer wears the Russian spiked helmet with a special cockade behind the chin strap.
Centre: Rifleman of a Caucasian rifle battalion. The long tunic, or demi-kaftan, was introduced for some units during the Crimea. This soldier also wears the "papacha" (fur cap) peculiar to Caucasian troops. His uniform is piped with red – the colour worn by all rifle units. Line troops wore white piping.
Right: Russian Lancer. His uniform was very similar to that worn by British Lancers. At Balaclava both sides mistook enemy lancers for their own. The distinctive Lancers' cap has a black waterproof cover.

Left: Rifleman of a "Strelkhovy" battalion with distinctive raspberry red shoulder straps and piping. Right: Russian Infantryman in greatcoat and forage cap. Both figures show the thick Russian overcoats. The heavily pleated back and the very long sleeves meant that one size of coat could be adjusted to fit different size men.

Above: Officers of the Dorsetshires. The numeral 39 on their blue forage caps proclaims these officers to be from the 39th Regiment of Foot. The swords and slung telescopes are appropriate to their rank, but some have covered their undress scarlet shell jackets with serviceable "Balaclava" jackets.

Near right above: A Highland Trio – Gardner, Mackenzie and Glen. The 42nd or Royal Highland Regiment of Foot made an impressive and colourful display, with bonnet, kilt and white sporran. More important, with battle honours at the Alma and Sebastopol, they had a fine reputation as fighting men. One is reminded of the vital part that Highlanders played, and the prominence they achieved, in so many overseas campaigns of the Victorian period, by the V.C. subsequently awarded to William Gardner (later colour-sergeant, on left) for gallantry in India.

Far right above: Sergeant William Russell of the Royal Horse Artillery.

Below right: L'Entente Cordiale. Photographer Roger Fenton had to work within definite limitations. His cumbersome equipment and the need for time exposures meant that action pictures were impossible. He therefore had to concentrate on camp scenes, posed groups and "V.I.P.s." Victorian susceptibilities formed another limitation: the horrors of war would have been unacceptable. After the grim reality described by William Russell, it was re-assuring to see that in off-duty hours English and French could fraternize in a convivial gathering over pipes and glasses!
(*All four pictures National Army Museum.*)

Turkish Artilleryman with an Infantryman in the background. In 1820 the Turkish Army had adopted European style uniforms. Both infantry and artillery wore blue coats trimmed with red and red fezes with blue tassels. In winter long grey or white cloaks or overcoats with hoods were worn. They were mostly armed with French smooth bore muskets.

The French and British officers had mixed feelings about their Turkish allies. They were usually described as fine men, well drilled and disciplined, but their uniforms were shoddy and they were badly armed and badly officered. Both their medical service and their commissariat were hopelessly disorganised.

General Staff Major of the Sardinian Expeditionary Force, with Sardinian Bersaglieri (Riflemen) in the background. The Piedmont troops (commonly called Sardinians) left their gay uniforms – blue coats and French-style shakos – at home, and the infantry went to the Crimea in grey overcoats and Italian fishermen's caps.The Bersaglieri wore their famous broad-brimmed hats with the plume of cock's feathers or a tasseled fez. The cavalry wore dark blue tunics, grey blue trousers and greatcoats and helmets or low shakos in yellow waterproof covers. The Piedmontese troops were very well equipped and trained and won the admiration of their allies. (See appendix.)

Cavalry N.C.O.s and Troopers. From left to right: Sergeant 8th Hussars, Trooper 17th Lancers, Sergeant 4th Dragoon Guards, Trooper 5th Dragoon Guards. (*Illustrated London News.*)

Cavalry Officers. From left to right: 1st Royal Dragoons, 13th Light Dragoons, 6th Inniskillin Dragoons and 11th Hussars. The latter regiment were Lord Cardigan's own and he lavished large sums of money on equipping them in a splendid fashion. They were known as the "Cherry pickers" after the colour of their trousers. (*Illustrated London News.*)

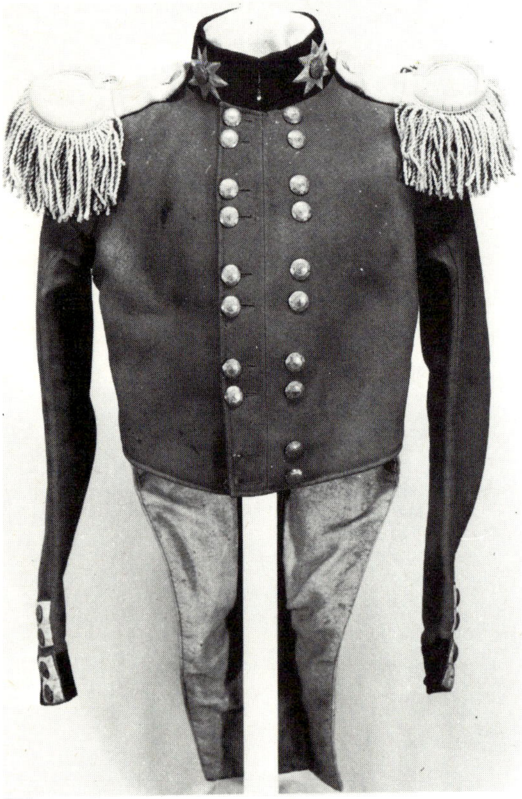

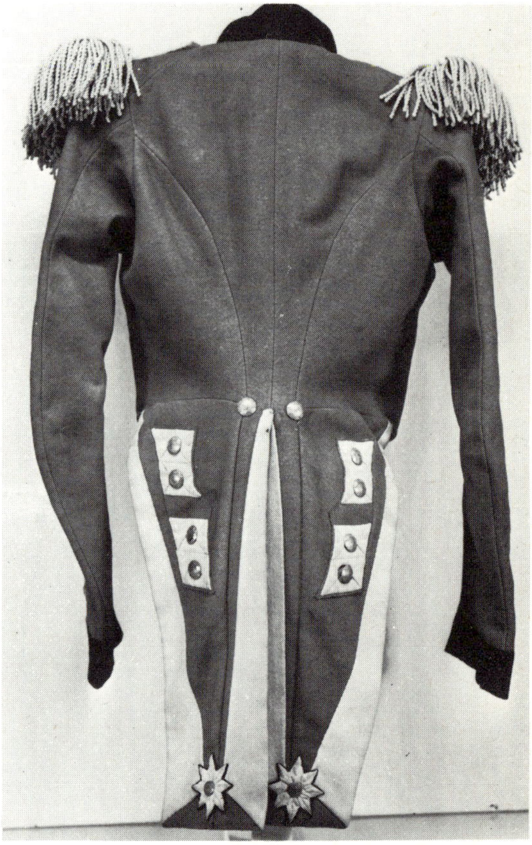

The double breasted coat was only introduced at the end of the war. The guards like their comrades in the line regiments wore the impractical and uncomfortable coatee illustrated here. The star badge and buttons in pairs indicate that it belongs to the 2nd or Coldstream Guards. (*National Army Museum.*)

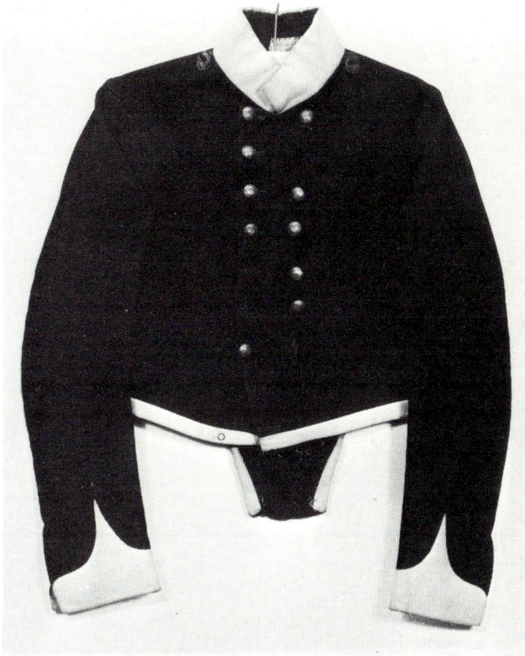

Above left: Helmet, 5th Dragoon Guards. This was the Albert Helmet, authorized in 1847 and in general use by 1850. The scroll around the VR in the centre gives the regimental title. Black plumes were general until 1855, when brass or gilt was replaced by white metal for the helmet.

Above right: Trooper's coatee, 13th Light Dragoons. It is dark blue with white cuffs, collar and turnbacks.

Below right: Forage cap of a trooper, 13th Light Dragoons.
(*All three pictures National Army Museum.*)

The French Army

Above and above right: The French army in the Crimea. From left to right the soldiers are as follows: Soldier of the line; Officer d'Etat Major; Spahis; Dragoon; Artilleryman; Hussar; Cantinière; Lancer; Engineer; Zouave; Chasseur de Vincennes; Carabineer; Chasseur d'Afrique; Guide. (*Illustrated London News.*)

Below right: A group of senior French officers. Note the dashing and rather comfortable uniforms. The French army was way ahead of the British in field equipment, tents, etc., and her soldiers, though rather casual by British standards, were tough and professional. These were the uniforms of the French army that so influenced those of the American troops during the Civil War of 1861-5. (*National Army Museum.*)

Above: Zouaves. The Zouaves were originally composed of native Algerian troops but by the time of the Crimean War they were made up of Europeans in North African style uniform. The Zouaves were light infantry and gained a fine reputation for bravery. The readiness of other armies, such as the Americans, to raise "Zouave" units, copying their style of uniform, can be seen as a compliment.

Right: Cantinière. Modern students of the U.S.A. army may comment sarcastically on the practice of taking the ice-cream wagon into action! Yet in the French army, from Napoleon's day, it was usual for wines and spirits to be available, and the regard paid to some of the practical sides of campaigning can be seen in their field kitchens and canteens. The attendants, often capable and personable women, had style—and sported a distinctive costume! (*Both pictures National Army Museum.*)

The Turkish Army

The Turkish ally. For nearly a year after autumn 1853, the Turks had fought their Russian opponents without assistance mostly along the Danube in territory which is now Rumania or Bulgaria. Their armies contained diverse elements, and their commanders likewise could be professional "mercenaries" from various eastern lands; but they fought with courage and resolution and were eminently successful. When the Crimean campaign developed, they did not figure so prominently, though again, when on their own at Eupatoria, they routed the Russian opposition with confidence.

Above left: Turkish artillery in overcoats with hoods and red fezzes. (*Illustrated London News.*)

Below left: Bashi-Bouzouks were irregular troops in the pay of the Sultan. They figured prominently in the Turkish operations against the Russians along the Danube in 1853-4. They were often a source of embarrassment to their Turkish chiefs and to their allies, because of their wanton pillaging and marauding, even at the expense of their own side. (*National Army Museum.*)

Above: Ismael Pasha and attendants. It was common practice for "foreigners" to find employment and achieve eminence in the Sultan's service. Ismael Pasha was a Circassian who rose from the ranks. These mercenaries conformed to Turkish customs, especially the practice of smoking the long pipe or chibouque. High-ranking officers rarely appeared without a small retinue of attendants, one of whom had the duty of carrying the chibouque. (*National Army Museum.*)

Captured Russian Equipment

Above: Helmet plate of the Russian 35th Infantry Regiment.
Below: A rather battered Russian bugle captured during the Crimean campaign.

Above: Helmet plate of the Russian 42nd Naval Detachment.
Below: A Russian Drum captured by the British 88th Regiment.
(*All four pictures National Army Museum*.)

Above: Russian infantryman's cartridge box.

Right: Russian "Pickelhaube" Helmet. This was the general service issue, made basically of tough black leather. The globe and spiked crest, the overlapping scales covering the chin-strap, and the helmet plate were metallic (gilt).
(*Both pictures National Army Museum.*)

The Alma

Left: The British attack on the heights of the Alma was the first major engagement of a British army since Waterloo. Conditions did not auger too well for success – until the very hour of battle men were still dropping out and dying of cholera; the landing only six days before had given no chance of acclimatization, the men (still in "full scarlet") had had to endure wet nights in the open and thirsty days under cloudless skies, Fast-moving Cossack patrols kept the British march south in view all the time; and the Russians, with well-placed batteries on the heights beyond the Alma and prepared positions on the steep river-bank, had reason to believe they could hold on for three or four weeks. However, in spite of huge Russian reserves in the rear, it was all over in three or four hours, thanks to the dash of the French against their left wing and the amazing gallantry and stubbornness of the British against the centre and right, where they carried the fight to the enemy across open ground and every kind of impediment under merciless fire.

Above: The field of Alma after the battle, sketched by an officer of the 21st, North British Fusileers.
(Both pictures Illustrated London News.)

The Charge of the Light Brigade

Above left: Lord Cardigan. A somewhat sleek and idealized portrayal of the leader of the Charge of the Light Brigade, though the exaggeration can be pardoned; he was apt to be larger than life! Spurning the signs of the enemy and followed by his trusted lancers and dragoons, he surges forward with urbane confidence, not even having to spur his superb mount.

High-handed and unpopular with his officers – he was tried before the House of Lords for duelling – his courage was never in question. Surviving the tragic charge, he rode back to his private yacht. (*National Army Museum.*)

Above right: Captain Lewis Edward Nolan. Rumour has not always dealt kindly with this gifted officer, who rode in great haste bearing the fateful and misunderstood message to Lord Lucan and Lord Cardigan, at Balaclava, which resulted in the Charge of the Light Brigade. His untimely death that afternoon – he was killed in the first salvo from the Russian guns – poses another query about the famous charge. Some reports insist that he realized the mistake only seconds before being hit, and was trying to head the charge in the intended direction. (*Illustrated London News.*)

Right: Cornet H. J. Wilkins, 11th Hussars. The 11th Hussars formed the second line in the famous Charge of the Light Brigade. This photo was taken in the spring of 1855 by Roger Fenton, Cornet Wilkins being a survivor from among "the gallant six hundred." Cornet was the most junior rank among cavalry officers, but true to cavalry traditions (Hussars in particular) his appearance was impeccable, in splendid full dress uniform of blue laced with gold, and the crimson trousers which distinguished the 11th Hussars. (*Ron Harris.*)

Casualties at the Charge of the Light Brigade.

Regiment	Present at Balaclava	Total Casualties
4th Light Dragoons	126	45
13th Light Dragoons	128	56
8th Hussars	115	41
11th Hussars	142	63
17th Lancers	147	77

The Charge of the Light Brigade

Below: The Charge of the Light Brigade at Balaclava. A courageous stand by the 93rd Highlanders stemmed the Russian advance on the allied base of Balaclava, and a charge by Scarlett's Heavy Brigade forced their cavalry back. Then came the hasty and vague order from Lord Raglan which was wrongly interpreted, causing Lord Cardigan to lead one of the most famous charges in history: nearly 700 men of the Light Brigade followed their impertubable commander into a veritable death-trap a mile and a half long – a valley flanked by Russian guns and troops, and sealed at its end by further batteries and cavalry. The Light Brigade was led by the 17th Lancers and the 13th Light Dragoons. These two regiments were followed by the 11th Hussars, the 4th Light Dragoons and the 8th Hussars. The painting by Caton Woodville is entitled "Charging an Army". (*National Army Museum.*)

Above right: The Chasseurs d'Afrique at Balaclava. After the Light Brigade had begun their advance and were visibly suffering casualties from the Russian cross-fire, a partial respite was gained by a furious and spirited charge by the Chasseurs d'Afrique against the Russian batteries on the allies' left. Though only 200 strong, they made a terrific impact, and added to their already fine reputation. (*Illustrated London News.*)

Below right: A group of Chasseurs d'Afrique. They were lightly armed troops. They were skilful horsemen and were regarded as an elite force.
(*National Army Museum.*)

Inkerman

Above: The repulse of the Russians at Inkerman. (*Illustrated London News.*)

Right: The Battle of Inkerman. Although Russian despatches tended to play it down as a "sortie", there is no denying the significance of Inkerman as a major battle and an allied victory. The British high command had evidence of an imminent Russian onslaught, but were surprised at the exact timing of it, in the early hours of a dark, foggy, drizzling morning on 5 November, across high ground above the Chernaya River near the ruins of Inkerman. The difficult conditions (for both sides), the huge numbers of Russian infantry, and the ravine-gullied terrain which split the fighting into several small "battles" – and which caused Inkerman to be known as "The Soldiers' Battle" – made central direction extremely difficult, while the Russians certainly suffered from deficient planning. The fighting, which lasted over twelve hours before the Russians retreated back into Sebastopol, showed characteristics that reccurred during the Crimean campaign – the solidity and doggedness of the British infantry (shown on the left) who took the first shock of attack, and the dash of their French allies (on the right) under General Bosquet. (*Illustrated London News.*)

Above left: Colonel Todleben was a famous name among military engineers. He was put in charge of Sebastopol's fortifications, although only thirty-five. With unusual drive and energy and a good eye for position and terrain, he was quick to take advantage of the cautious approach of the allies in the autumn of 1854. Without the time to make stone emplacements, he showed what could be done with earth in the shape of huge ramparts, supporting and hiding up to 1,000 guns. After the siege he was made a general. (*Illustrated London News.*)

Above right: General Niel. This eminent French engineer officer was strongly of the opinion that the correct strategy for the allies should have been to invest Sebastopol completely, on all sides. However, he did not reach the Crimea in time to alter the basic plan, although the fact that he had won the Emperor Napoleon over to his way of thinking, and that the latter was disposed to take over the supreme command, did make things difficult for Canrobert and Pélissier. (*Illustrated London News.*)

Left: General Bosquet. Both personally and professionally he made as great a contribution to the successes of the allies as any of the commanders. Affable and approachable, he was accommodating over problems of supply, and with his aides and staff (Capt. Dampière here) was deservedly popular. None knew the terrain as well as he did, and he showed a Napoleonic keenness in being in close touch with the fighting. Gravely wounded in his greatest success, the taking of Malakoff, he survived to become a senator and a marshal. (*National Army Museum.*)

Sebastopol

Above: The road to Sebastopol. Although the long siege inevitably showed many of the features of static warfare, yet the steady advancing of the allied line, and the insatiable demand for more of everything for the thousands of men encamped north of Balaclava, meant that transport and communication were ever-present problems. Before the seven miles of rail linking harbour and upland were finished, recourse was had to every possible means of moving supplies, causing great variety in motive-power, in driver, and in load. Mules, horses, oxen and even camels played their part, carrying or pulling guns, ammunition, food, and bundles of fascines for the earthworks—and if a few soldiers managed to hitch-hike, it was a just recompense for the wet days when they too had to lend a shoulder! (*Illustrated London News.*)

The siege of Sebastopol. As 1855 progressed, the allies pushed their front line of entrenchments forward across the plateau towards the anchorage and the military installations which were mainly along its southern side (see below right): A ring of trenches and rifle-pits, batteries and strong-points, were the chief physical obstacles to advance. The two most important strongpoints were the Malakoff and the Redan, largely earth structures with emplacements protected by sandbags and gabions.

The Russians did not defend their base only by passive occupation of their defences. They inflicted constant and numerous casualties by their gunnery, and sorties on various scales were resorted to in the eleven months of the siege. But towards the end, when the allies had pushed their guns closer to the town, the Russians had to summon all their resolve to carry on in the increasing destruction and with appalling casualties.

An end to the ordeal was inevitable after the French so brilliantly stormed the Malakoff in a few minutes on 8 September. They were well briefed, well prepared with scaling ladders, and showed immense dash. The failure of the British to take the Redan was disappointing, although great courage was shown by the 2nd and Light Divisions in entering and holding on for nearly two hours, when insufficient support necessitated withdrawal. But the badly mauled defenders abandoned the works a few hours later—as they did the whole of ravaged Sebastopol. (*Illustrated London News.*)

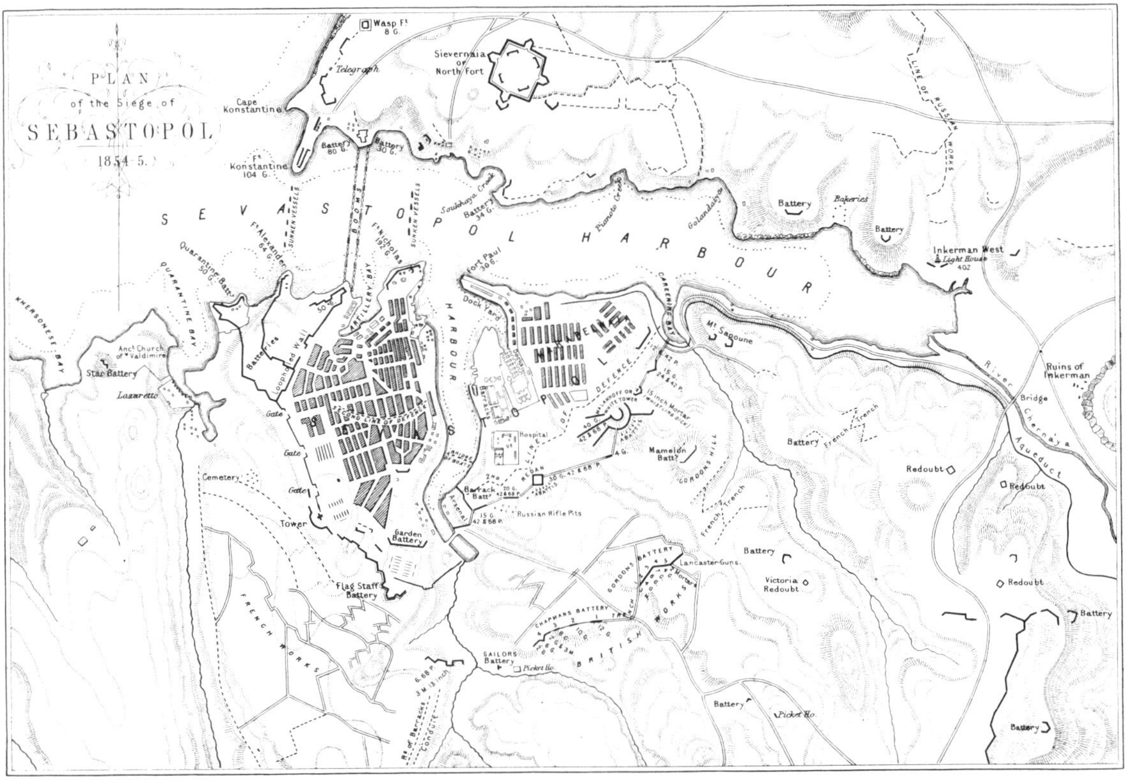
PLAN
of the Siege of
SEBASTOPOL
1854-5.
Wasp Ft
8 G.
Sievernaia
or
North Fort
Telegraph
Cape
Konstantine
Battery
80 G.
Battery
30 G.
Konstantine
104 G.
SEVASTOPOL HARBOUR
Quarantine Bay
Quarantine Batt.
50 G.
Ft Alexander
64 G.
Ft Nicholas
192 G.
Fort Paul
30 G.
Artillery Bay
Dock Yard
Hospital
Barrack
Arsenal
Mamelon Batt.
Gordons Hill
Mt Sapoune
Star Battery
Lazaretto
Cemetery
Gate
Tower
Garden Battery
Flag Staff Battery
French Works
British Works
Sailors Battery
Picket Ho.
Chapmans Battery
Gordons Battery
Lancaster Guns
Victoria Redoubt
Redoubt
Battery
Bakeries
Inkerman West
Light House
Ruins of Inkerman
Bridge
River Chernaya
Aqueduct
Line of Russian Works
Russian Rifle Pits
French Trench
Khersonese Bay
Ancient Church of St Valdimir
Sunken Vessels
Booms

Above: An allied battery bombarding Sebastopol. (*Illustrated London News.*)

Above right: The French storm the Malakoff. (*Illustrated London News.*)

Below right: The interior of the Redan, September 1855. Even in ruins one can conceive of the strength of the giant earthwork which engineer Todleben had designed and erected in less than a fortnight across the approached to Sebastopol. A precipitous ditch was surmounted by steep banks topped by gabions (stout wicker containers packed with earth), and sandbags. Guns mounted in each of the embrasures commanded a wide field of fire, and the gunners were protected by mantelets (tough rope mats slung across the embrasure, with a collar through which the gun protruded). A collapsed one can be seen on the left, adjoining a stack of powder cartridges for the guns. The "amenities" included a bomb and mortar-proof shelter. (*Illustrated London News.*)

The British ambulance **(top)** was a four-wheeled carriage drawn by six mules in the charge of three postboys clad in Artillery undress uniform. Six slightly wounded could sit under the canopy in front, while the body of the carriage contained four berths for the more gravely wounded. Thus began a journey to the base hospital at Scutari across the Black Sea. British ambulances were often unavailable, or arrived late, or the tracks and terrain did not suit wheeled vehicles. By contrast the relative simplicity of the French system **(above)** was seen to be far superior. For the gravely sick or injured, a mule would be fitted with two long, canopied "cradles", slung like panniers on either side, and led by a service-man (familiar with the ways of mules) dressed and armed like an infantryman. For the slightly wounded, a mule would have a chair with foot-rest slung on either side. There seems little doubt that the French plan was more practical and professional, and produced less discomfort.
(*Both pictures Illustrated London News.*)

Right: Some of the wounded at least had the means of making their stories realistic. These Crimean veterans hold the shot that wounded them.
(*Illustrated London News.*)

Above: The barrack hospital at Scutari.

Left: Florence Nightingale (1820-1910) worked in the Black Sea theatre of operations from October 1854 until the final departure of British troops in July 1856. Her work for men, above all for "common soldiers," had to be done in a world dominated by men and the shortcomings of men, against a public opinion that was inclined to look askance at such activity by a woman. She was inspired by compassion, but re-inforced by practical knowledge, an iron will and the necessary drive in organisation.

Right: The "Lady with a Lamp" makes her evening round of the overcrowded wards at Scutari. The large disused barracks which the Turks had placed at her disposal was not an ideal hospital, but to the sick and wounded who had spent four days untended on a transport across the Black Sea it was a haven, even though in the autumn of 1854 there were 10,000 of them in the space for 2,000, and many lay in the passage-ways without mattresses and blankets. Proper sanitation and hygiene were absent until Florence Nightingale set to work to bring order out of chaos; and as for supplies, one of her nurses wrote, after a month of superhuman effort, "We have not seen a drop of milk, and the bread is extremely sour, the butter most filthy . . . the meat is more like moist leather than food." Perseverance ultimately stemmed the appalling death-rate, and in 1855 three base-hospitals were set up in the Crimea itself. (*All three pictures Illustrated London News.*)

William Russell

William Russell of "The Times". Russell was in the Crimea from the start. His newspaper, already famous for "finding news" independently of government "hand-outs", printed his trenchant reports and letters exposing the muddle and mismanagement that made the autumn and winter of 1854-5 so terrible for the troops. The reports were at first denied, but the casualty lists and subsequent events bore him out and justified his attempt to shock the national conscience. The first great war correspondent, he brought honour and dignity to his profession. (*Illustrated London News.*)

Table of Dates

1815 Battle of Waterloo. The "Concert of Europe" and the Metternich System.
1825 Nicholas succeeds his brother Alexander as Czar of Russia.
1829 Treaty of Adrianople.
1830 July Revolution in Paris. Louis-Philippe replaces the Bourbons.
1832 Russia gains partial protectorate of Wallachia and Moldavia. Mehemet Ali's success against the Sultan, who accepts Russian mediation.
1833 Treaty of Unkiar Skelessi. Russia gains military and naval advantages.
1837 Queen Victoria's accession.
1840 Return of Napoleon's remains from St Helena to France.
1841 Treaty of the Dardanelles, largely preserving the "status quo" after the Sultan's failure to regain Syria: a success for Palmerston.
1848 The Year of Revolutions. Louis-Philippe replaced by the Second Republic in France.
1849 Political chaos in France; emergence of Louis Napoleon. Russia aids Austria to subdue Magyar rising.
1851 End of the Second Republic. The Great Exhibition in Hyde Park.
1852 Louis Napoleon assumes title of Emperor.

1853

October Turkey declares war on Russia.

1854

March Britain and France declare war in support of Turkey. Allied squadron sent to Baltic, and troops to Varna on Black Sea coast.

July Russian army withdraws from Wallachia and Moldavia after reverses on lower Danube.

September Allied expeditionary force land in Crimea. Battle of the Alma. Main Russian army leaves Sebastopol. British occupy Balaclava.

October Return of Russian forces to Sebastopol, strengthened by Todleben. Siege of Sebastopol begins — first attack by sea bombardment. Florence Nightingale leaves for Scutari. Battle of Balaclava.

November Battle of Inkerman. Great storms cause serious losses.

1855

January Kingdom of Piedmont joins the allies.

February French take over responsibility for the Malakhov.

March Death of Czar Nicholas. Russians occupy the Mamelon. The Great Sortie. Abortive peace conference in Vienna.

April The Second Bombardment of Sebastopol. Railway from Balaclava in operation.

May Landing of Piedmontese troops. Three hospitals in Crimea. Canrobert relinquishes command of French troops to Pélissier. Sea expedition to Kerch.

June The Third Bombardment. Relative failure of ensuing attack, though French take the Mamelon and British the Quarries. Further attack on 18th a costly failure.

August Russian attempt to break the siege in the Chernaya River attack — a failure.

September Final allied attack after sustained bombardment. French storm the Malakhov. Sebastopol evacuated.

1856

March The Peace of Paris.

Appendix — Piedmont

Although Piedmont did not officially enter the war until January 1855, and the soldiers of the Expeditionary Force did not arrive until May, yet officers from various Piedmont Army Corps were present from the autumn of 1854. They came with the full concurrence of the allies, and though simply called "observers" there was no secret as to the real reason for their presence — preparing for the arrival of the Piedmont troops. (They were not "technical experts" installing equipment, in the modern sense of the term!) Their presence clearly shows how Prime Minister Cavour was fully committed to uniting Italy under the House of Savoy by expelling the Austrians with military help from one or both of the western allies. Two of the North Italian officers, a Staff Major and a Lieutenant of Cavalry, were with the British Cavalry Division on the day of Balaclava, and asked permission to participate in the celebrated charge, almost certainly in the first line. Staff Major Govone came through successfully, but Lieut. Landriani was severly wounded and captured.